D0894569

WITHDRAWN

Profiles in Greek and Roman Mythology

DIONYSUS

Mitchell Lane
PUBLISHERS

P.O. Box 196
Hockessin, Delaware 19707
Visit us on the web: www.mitchelllane.com
Comments? email us: mitchelllane@mitchelllane.com

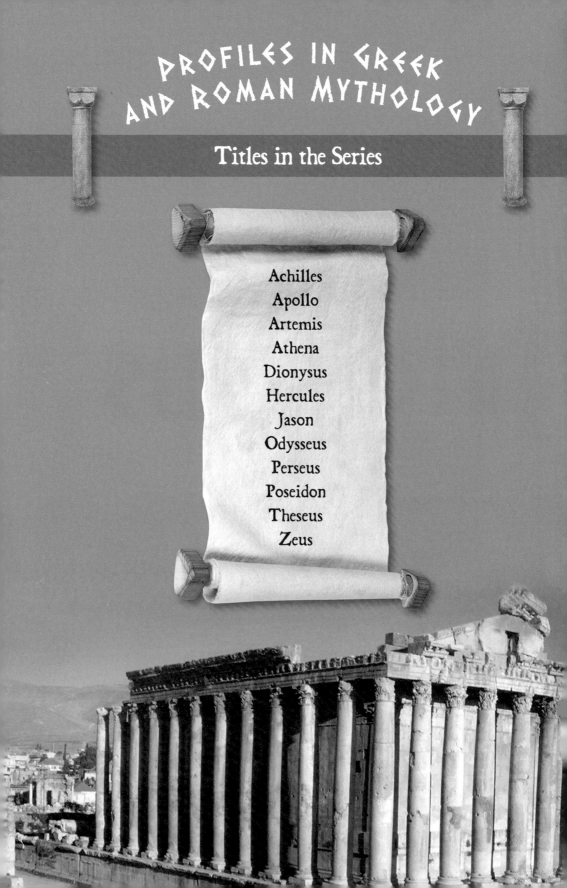

PROFILES IN GREEK AND ROMAN MYTHOLOGY

Titles in the Series

Profiles in Greek and Roman Mythology

DIONYSUS

Russell Roberts

Mitchell Lane
PUBLISHERS

P.O. Box 196
Hockessin, Delaware 19707
Visit us on the web: www.mitchelllane.com
Comments? email us: mitchelllane@mitchelllane.com

Mitchell Lane
PUBLISHERS

Copyright © 2008 by Mitchell Lane Publishers. All rights reserved. No part of this book may be reproduced without written permission from the publisher. Printed and bound in the United States of America.

Printing   2   3   4   5   6   7   8   9

Library of Congress Cataloging-in-Publication Data
Roberts, Russell, 1953–
    Dionysus / by Russell Roberts.
        p. cm. — (Profiles in Greek and Roman mythology)
    Includes bibliographical references and index.
    ISBN 978-1-58415-557-7 (library bound)
    I. Dionysus (Greek deity)—Juvenile literature. I. Title.
BL820.B2R63 2007
398.20938'01—dc22
                                                                            2007000770

ABOUT THE AUTHOR: Russell Roberts has written and published nearly 40 books for adults and children on a variety of subjects, including baseball, memory power, business, New Jersey history, and travel. He has written numerous books for Mitchell Lane Publishers, including *Nathaniel Hawthorne, Thomas Jefferson, Holidays and Celebrations in Colonial America, Daniel Boone, The Lost Continent of Atlantis, Nostradamus,* and *Athena.* The dual nature of Dionysus and his paradoxical effect on people presents a worthy challenge to any writer to explore. He lives in Bordentown, New Jersey, with his family and a fat, fuzzy, and crafty calico cat named Rusti.

CREDITS: pp. 6, 32—Barbara Marvis; p. 9—Exekias/Antikensammlungen; p. 12—Carracci; p. 15—Bernard Picart; p. 16—Olympia Museum, Greece; p. 20—Guido Reni; p. 23—Nicolas Poussin; p. 25—French royal collections–in the Louvre collections since 1800; p. 26—Arnold Böcklin; p. 28—Diego Velásquez de Silva; p. 30—Caravaggio; p. 36—Giovanni Battista Pittoni; p. 38—Tizian/National Gallery, London; p. 40—Francesco de Mura.

PUBLISHER'S NOTE: Portions of this story have been retold using dialogue as an aid to readability. The dialogue is based on the author's extensive research and approximates what is related in the myths. Documentation of his research is contained on page 46.

    The internet sites referenced herein were active as of the publication date. Due to the fleeting nature of some web sites, we cannot guarantee they will all be active when you are reading this book.

    To reflect current usage, we have chosen to use the secular era designations BCE ("before the common era") and CE ("of the common era") instead of the traditional designations BC ("before Christ") and AD (*anno Domini,* "in the year of the Lord").

TABLE OF CONTENTS

Profiles in Greek and Roman Mythology

DIONYSUS

Dionysus, the Greek god of wine, holds aloft a bunch of grapes, the fruit from which wine is made.

DIONYSUS

CHAPTER 1

A Bad Day to Be a Pirate

One sunny day near ancient Greece, a pirate ship was sailing across the sea. The winds were light, the sea calm, the sun bright, there was no hint of storms or foul weather—and the pirates on board ship were in a festive mood. It was a good day to be a pirate. As the ship cruised along the coast, the pirates spotted a young man walking along the shore. He was quite handsome, with dark eyes and long brown hair flowing down to his shoulders. His clothes were nice, especially his lovely purple cloak. He looked like the son of a king or some other rich man.

The pirates decided to kidnap the youth and hold him for ransom. Several of them hurried ashore, grabbed the young man as he was walking on the beach, and brought him back to the ship. Once they were all back on board, the pirates grinned happily, thinking about the nice, fat ransom this young man would bring.

The pirates decided to tie him up so that they would not have to guard him constantly. Thick rope was brought over.

As the pirates began tying the young man up, a remarkable thing happened. They found they could not tie their prisoner's hands and feet together. No matter how tightly they pulled the ropes and made the knots, the ropes loosened and slid off. The pirates began muttering to each other: What was going on here?

The young man said nothing. He merely smiled as he watched the pirates with his dark eyes.

Then one of the pirates had a terrible thought. "This is not a mortal youth, but a god!" he cried. "We have kidnapped a god! We must release him at once and beg his forgiveness!"

The pirate captain shook his head. "He's no god!" he snapped. "The ropes must be too wet to hold securely. Now let's raise the sail and leave here."

When the pirates raised the sail, another amazing thing happened. The wind came and filled the sails, and the ship should have moved— yet it stayed perfectly still in the water.

Then rivers of wine streamed down the sail. A thick green grapevine began growing all over the ship. It grew rapidly, curling around the ship's wheel and other parts. Giant white flowers opened on the vine.

At last the pirates knew the truth. This *was* a god. All the pirates fearfully looked over at him.

Pirates were a scourge even in ancient Greece. Trade was prosperous along the Aegean Sea, which met the Mediterranean Sea around Crete. The pirates in the Dionysus story would have known these waters well.

The young man was gone. In his place was a ferocious lion, snarling and growling and set to pounce. In another part of the ship, a bear roamed, killing everyone it found.

Screaming, the pirates leaped overboard into the sea, trying to swim for safety. As each man jumped into the water, he was changed into a dolphin. This explains why the dolphin is like a fish, yet is extremely close to being human.

The inside of a kylix, or wine cup, from around 540 BCE shows Dionysus in the pirates' ship, with vines growing from the mast. The pirates have already turned into dolphins. One of the things the tale of Dionysus and the pirates was trying to explain may have been why dolphins have some very humanlike characteristics.

Finally, the only pirate who was left was the one who had first guessed that their prisoner was a god. The lion vanished and in its place stood the young man again.

"Have no fear," he told the trembling pirate, "for I am the god Dionysus, and am pleased with how you so quickly identified me. I will not cause you to suffer the same fate as your friends." So the pirate's life was spared.

This is the most popular version of a tale told about the Greek god Dionysus (dy-oh-NY-sus).[1] In other versions, Dionysus hired a pirate ship to take him somewhere, but once again the pirates did not know who he was and decided to sail to Asia and sell the young man as a slave. Realizing their intentions, Dionysus transformed the mast and oars of the ship into snakes so that they could not be used. He then filled the ship with ivy and the sound of flutes playing, which drove the sailors insane. They jumped into the sea and were changed into dolphins, or, in other versions, got into a small boat and rowed away.

No matter which version of the story is followed, it was still a bad day to be a pirate. But who was this god who was capable of such violence and anger one moment, and then could be kind and forgiving the next?

Piracy

When we think of pirates, we think of them with large hats and colorful clothes, shooting pistols, and saying things like "Avast, ye hearties!" These kinds of images come from what is commonly known as the Golden Age of Piracy in the Caribbean Sea in the late seventeenth and early eighteenth centuries. In fact, pirates were around for much longer than that—even as far back as the days of ancient Greece.

Eighteenth-century pirates

In ancient times, pirates constantly attacked ships on the Mediterranean Sea and sometimes even organized raids onto land. They were often considered honorable men—as compared to the negative manner in which they were later viewed. They would attack a ship or a city and bring home things like food, water, and clothing to the poorer folks among their own people. Pirates were admired because they helped the less fortunate.

However, not everyone appreciated their "generosity." Piracy was supposedly the reason that Minos (MY-nohs), King of Crete, established a navy. He grew tired of losing so many ships to pirates. Another Greek city-state, Rhodes, also used its sea power to keep pirate activities in check.

When the Romans defeated the kingdom of Rhodes, they accidentally removed what had been a restraining influence on pirate activities in the Mediterranean Sea. The Roman Empire replaced Greece as the dominant world power, but it had a terrible time with pirates. The pirates raided both ships and cities in the Roman Empire without mercy. Since Rome needed the food and goods that these ships carried, the pirates were a serious threat to the health and well-being of the empire.

Finally, beginning in 67 BCE, a Roman military genius named Pompey led a campaign against the pirates, and soon had virtually freed the entire Mediterranean from their grasp. Then, as the Roman Empire weakened, pirates again began to flourish. However, it wasn't until the discovery of the New World and the rich trading routes it opened that pirates once again became a terror on the high seas.

Zeus, the king of the gods, and Hera, his queen. Although Zeus loved Hera, he could not stop himself from becoming involved with other women. Dionysus was the result of one of Zeus' affairs.

DIONYSUS

CHAPTER 2

Lord of the Vine

Dionysus is the Greek god of wine and winemaking. The Greeks also considered him a promoter of civilization, a lawgiver, a lover of peace, and the god who watched over agriculture and the theater.

The story of Dionysus' birth and childhood—and subsequent discovery of wine and winemaking—led some to feel that he was a new god. But was he? Or was he, in fact, an old deity brought over to Greece from another country?

The Strange Birth and Childhood of Dionysus

According to the Greeks, the story of Dionysus began with his mortal mother. Semele (SEH-muh-lee) was the beautiful daughter of Cadmus, the king of Thebes. Zeus (ZOOS), the king of the gods, saw her and fell in love with her. He decided that he had to be with her. The only problem was that Zeus was already married—to Hera (HAYR-uh), the extremely jealous queen of the gods. Hera knew that Zeus had often fallen in love with pretty mortal women, so she was always keeping an eye on him. She knew right away when Zeus and Semele became involved.

Besides being jealous, Hera was also vindictive. When she found out about Semele, she decided to take revenge on her.

Disguised as an old woman, Hera went to visit Semele. During the visit, she and Semele talked about many things. Finally, very innocently, the old woman asked the young girl—who was pregnant—who and where her husband was.

"My husband is the mighty Zeus, King of the Gods and father of my child," Semele answered proudly.

"Oh, dearie," said the old woman, with pity, "I've known many men who claim that they are the mighty Zeus. I think it's best to be certain. Why don't you ask him to show himself to you in all his god-like glory?" Then she walked away, and Semele was left alone to think about her words.

The next time Zeus came to see Semele, she asked him if he would grant her one wish. Zeus loved the girl very much, so he swore by the River Styx—a very sacred oath to the gods—that he would grant her any wish she desired.

"Reveal yourself to me in all your godlike splendor," said Semele.

When Zeus heard her wish, he was horrified and begged her to change her mind. He knew that no mortal could bear the sight of him as the mightiest god of all, a hundred times more brilliant than the sun, with his flashing thunderbolts. But Hera had done her work well. She had planted the seeds of doubt so deeply into Semele's mind and heart that nothing could persuade her to change her wish.

With a heavy heart, Zeus granted her wish. He came to her in all his glory, with blinding light and fire.

As Hera knew, no mortal could gaze upon a god this way. Upon seeing him, Semele caught fire and burned to a cinder. Zeus could only sadly watch as her spirit fluttered down to Hades (HAY-deez), the land of the dead.

However, he could and did rescue their baby, which dropped out of Semele's body as it burned. A thick column of ivy appeared and blocked the infant from the blinding light and fire of Zeus—otherwise he might well have perished too. Since the infant was not yet ready to be born, Zeus sewed him under the skin of his own thigh. When it was time for the birth, the baby sprang from Zeus's thigh as the immortal god Dionysus. This is a very popular version of the story of Dionysus' birth.[1]

In another, Cadmus, the father of Semele, became very angry with her because of her relationship with Zeus. He shut her up in a chest and threw it into the ocean. By the time the chest drifted ashore, Semele was dead. The baby inside her, however, was still alive. Ino, Semele's sister, appeared and was given the baby to raise. This story comes from Prasiae, a region that may have been another Greek city-state, but whose exact location in ancient times seems uncertain.[2]

There is still another version of Dionysus' birth that is much more violent. In it, Zeus again has an affair, this time with Persephone (pur-SEH-fuh-nee), the bride of Hades, the lord of the Underworld. She had the baby, and once again Hera flew into a jealous rage, but this time her anger turned murderous. She sent some Titans to kill the child. This they did by attracting the baby to them with toys, then tearing him limb from limb. Too late Zeus saw what was happening, and drove the Titans away with his thunderbolts. All that was left of the child was the heart, which one of the other gods—perhaps

In Bernard Picart's eighteenth-century engraving *Zeus and Semele,* Semele pays the price for becoming involved with Hera's husband.

Athena (uh-THEE-nuh)—saved. Zeus ground the heart into powder and slipped it into Semele's drink. She became pregnant and gave birth to Dionysus.

In all of these versions, Dionysus has two mothers: Semele and Zeus in the first two, and Persephone and Semele in the third. For that reason, Dionysus is often given the epithet *Dimetor,* which means "two mothers." He is referred to as "twice-born" for this same reason.

After the baby was born, Zeus realized that he could not bring up the child with the very jealous Hera around. He gave the baby to Ino, Semele's sister.

However, Hera's jealousy was still not satisfied. She caused Ino to become insane, and Zeus once again had to take the baby. This time, he entrusted the child to Hermes, fleet messenger of the gods, with wings on his shoes and on his helmet. He instructed Hermes to bring the baby boy someplace where he would be safe from Hera. Hermes carried the child all the way to the valley of Nysa—far from Olympus. Hermes left the child with the Maenads (MAY-nadz), the nymphs who lived there.

Nysa was very green, with animals such as tigers and leopards roaming about. In one part of it, large bunches of purple grapes grew. Dionysus found the grapes and eventually discovered how to make wine from their juices.

When he was a young man, Dionysus went out into the world to share this amazing new gift of wine and winemaking with humanity. He dressed in beautiful purple robes to show his relationship with the grape and wine. Everywhere he went, he was celebrated as a new god. Watching all this from Mount Olympus, Zeus was very pleased.

A fourth-century sculpture depicts Hermes taking baby Dionysus to Nysa, the land of the Maenads.

Eventually, Zeus decided that Dionysus should be brought up to Mount Olympus to live among the gods. Hera said that she would never share Mount Olympus with this son of a mortal woman, but Zeus roared in anger and pounded his great fist, and Hera fell quiet.

When Dionysus came up to Mount Olympus, there were only twelve thrones in the great hall of the gods, and all were taken up by other gods. Hestia (HES-tee-uh), goddess of the hearth, got up from her throne and offered it to Dionysus.

"I need no throne," she said. "My place is at the hearth."

Before seating himself among the gods, Dionysus asked to go down to Hades, the land of the dead, so that he could see his mother. Zeus not only allowed Dionysus to do this, but he also permitted him to bring her up to Olympus. After all, she was the mother of a god. Dionysus gladly did so. For ever after, Semele and Dionysus lived on Mount Olympus.

By Land or By Sea

It is often thought that the followers and worship of Dionysus came from the land of Thrace (a large country that is today part of Turkey or Bulgaria). People migrating to Greece from that area brought the idea and concept of the god with them. But according to Dionysus scholar Walter Otto, worship of the god might have been brought to Greece by people who sailed across the Aegean Sea from Phrygia (another area that is thought to be part of modern-day Turkey).[3]

To support this theory, Otto cites evidence that in early festivals of Dionysus, the god first appeared in the celebration on board a ship set on wheels so that it could move on dry land, much like a modern-day float in a parade. Certainly much of Dionysus' life was tied to water. In one version of his birth, his mother is imprisoned in a chest that is thrown into the sea. Later on, as he travels across the world spreading his gift of wine and winemaking, he runs away from King Lycurgus (ly-KUR-gus) by disappearing into the sea. Some researchers feel that having Dionysus so intimately involved with water is a key to his origin.[4]

Otto also felt that the name of Dionysus came from the place where he was raised: Nysa. He thought that Nysa got its name from its inhabitants, who were called the Nysia. According to Otto, the name Dionysus came from the word *Dio-nysos,* which roughly translates as "the divine Nysos."[5]

Hera and Dionysus

Besides Hera's other attacks against Dionysus, there is also a story in which she causes him to become insane. (He is eventually cured.) It is possible that Hera's hatred of Dionysus is a reflection of how some people opposed the spread of winemaking among countries in Europe, Asia, and North Africa.

However, there is more than symbolism behind Hera's intense dislike of Dionysus. Hera represented the safe and stable institution of marriage. To her, all was right when women married and remained home to faithfully serve their husbands. Dionysus was the opposite of that. He signified the wild and the uninhibited in women. When he and his wine arrived, women left their homes and families and became Maenads, or followers of Dionysus. In their wild, wine-infused celebrations, Maenads danced, sang, cavorted, and even killed. They were not safe, stable women. So Hera hated Dionysus and all he represented.

Dionysus

Wine was not invented by the Greeks. Rather, it may have come from the island of Crete in jars. As much as Hera—or people in general—tried to stop Dionysus and his wine culture from spreading, it was a doomed effort. Grape cultivation and winemaking soon spread all over the known world. Eventually, around the end of the fifth century BCE, winemaking had become so popular that Dionysus actually replaced Hera as one of the twelve gods on Mount Olympus. The triumph of wine was complete.

The Wrath of Hera

In all of Greek mythology, no woman was as jealous as Hera . . . and no woman was more vicious when it came time for revenge.

Hera was the wife of Zeus, the king of the gods, so she was the queen of the universe. Even though he was married, Zeus often had affairs with other women. This drove Hera crazy with jealousy. She often took revenge on both the woman Zeus favored and the child the affair created—like Dionysus.

In fact, Hera got angry with *anybody* who helped Zeus cheat on her. For a time, a nymph named Echo was given the job of distracting Hera from Zeus' affairs by leading the queen away and praising her. Hera eventually discovered the trick and got mad at Echo. She made Echo able to speak only the words of others. (From this comes the modern word *echo*.)

The nymph, Echo, offended Hera by keeping her talking, which prevented her from spying on Zeus.

Another of Zeus' girlfriends was Leto (LEE-toh). When Hera found out Leto was pregnant with Zeus' child, she was so furious that she forbade Leto from giving birth on any part of the land or island at sea. Leto finally got around this by finding the floating island of Delos, which because it was floating was neither land nor sea.

Io was another female with whom Zeus had an affair. He had to change Io into a white heifer to disguise her from Hera. Not to be deceived, Hera demanded that Zeus give her the heifer as a present. She had Argus, who had 100 eyes, constantly watch her. After Zeus had Hermes kill Argus, Hera sent a gadfly to sting Io and drive her almost crazy. Thus was Io fated to wander the earth.

In another revenge story, Lamia (LAA-mee-uh) had children by Zeus. Hera killed their children and turned Lamia into a monster. The morale of all these stories seems clear: Don't cross Hera!

Dionysus was often shown as a bearded old man or a handsome youth. Since the god also symbolized rebirth, some artists, such as Guido Reni in 1623, painted him as a baby.

DIONYSUS

CHAPTER 3

Origins and Friends

Like other gods of Greek mythology, it is possible that Dionysus evolved from several other gods that existed in earlier civilizations. As he evolved, and new characteristics were attributed to him, he gradually became more than just the god of wine.

One theory about the origins of Dionysus is that he was a mixture of three gods: Sabazius (sah-BAY-zee-us) from Phrygia, the Lydian god Bassareus (buh-SAYR-ee-us), and Zagreus (ZAA-groos) from Crete. It is possible that the many stories about Dionysus reflect his numerous origins.[1]

Sabazius was a god from Phrygia. He was one of the supreme gods, somewhat comparable to Zeus. A major link to the character of Dionysus is that very savage, primitive festivals were held in Sabazius' honor. These were called the Sabazia. There are very similar in style and actions to those danced by the Maenads and others in honor of Dionysus. There is even a reference to Sabazius keeping the not-yet-ready-to-be-born Dionysus in his thigh until the moment of birth arrived.

The Dionysus link to the god possibly called Bassareus has to do with the battles that Dionysus fought and won on his travels throughout the world. Bassareus was reportedly a warlike god with many conquests from the region known as Lydia, which is again part of modern-day Turkey. The many conquests of Dionysus, as he journeyed to other lands, may have come from Bassareus.

Another potential link to Bassareus is that Dionysus sometimes had the epithet of "Bassareus" when he was depicted as wearing a long robe in an Asian fashion. In addition, sometimes his followers were also called Bassarids.

Dionysus' identification with the god Zagreus from Crete is strong. In a story about his birth, Dionysus Zagreus was the son of Zeus and such as herbs and berries, and milk from wild mountain goats. They slept not in enclosed structures on soft beds, but on grass and pine needles, with a sky full of stars and the moon as their only illumination. When they awoke, they bathed in a crystal-clear stream or brook, with the water gurgling all about them. Their minds were clean and pure. They were free of the noise, dust, and dirt of the city.

When described in that manner, there is much to like about the Maenads. They lived an uncomplicated life, free of routines and schedules. Their time was spent outdoors. It seems a peaceful, idyllic existence.

But the Maenads had another side, and that is the horrible frenzy that gripped them, causing them to kill. No one was safe from the Maenads in their wine frenzy, not even their own children. They were out of their heads with lust and fury.

These two concepts so widely different—peaceful joy and murderous rage—were critical to the worship of Dionysus. He brought either one to his followers—happiness or sorrow. It is this duality that is one of the most fascinating aspects of Dionysus.

Dual Dionysus

Even in the most common stories about the birth, childhood, and life of Dionysus, the paradoxical nature of this god can be seen. It can also be seen in the story about the pirates. On the one hand, Dionysus is kind-hearted and attractive, almost beautiful. He lets them try to tie him up instead of fighting them. On the other hand, he is ferocious and fearful. He not only causes a bear to appear on the pirate ship, but he himself turns into a lion.

Some scholars believe that having Dionysus act in two seemingly contradictory ways was how the Greeks dealt with the dual nature of drinking alcoholic beverages. Wine can make a person happy and pleasant, and it can also make them angry and dangerous. Drinking wine can seem good to some people at first; as they drink it, they may become confident, self-assured, and vain, even boastful. They feel a confidence they usually don't have when they are not drinking. However, these so-called benefits quickly become negatives. The more people drink, the less pleasant they feel. As they slide into drunkenness, the false confidence and self-assuredness that they first felt vanishes. They become unable to perform simple tasks. They cannot think or act clearly. They may become violent and mean. They often get sick to the stomach.

Since wine affects people in two vastly different ways, it was only natural that the god of wine also be paradoxical. He could be good and he could be harmful, just like those affected by wine. As Greek mythology scholar Edith Hamilton said: "The reason that Dionysus was so different at one time from another was because of this double nature of wine and so of the god of wine. He was man's benefactor and he was man's destroyer."[4]

Silenus

Among the figures who followed Dionysus from place to place—known as his retinue—was the character of Silenus (sy-LEE-nus). Silenus was a fat, bald, old man who was always drunk. He rode behind Dionysus on a donkey, and often swayed back and forth on it as if he were about to fall off. He was usually saved from doing so by Satyrs (SAY-turs)—horned, half-human woodland spirits with legs and feet like goats. They were also part of the retinue of Dionysus.

Silenus, even though he was always drunk, was nevertheless very cheerful. He also was extremely smart. In the god's younger days, Silenus had been his teacher. It was he who filled Dionysus' head with wisdom as he was growing up. There was almost nothing that Silenus did not know.

Silenus was Dionysus' friend, teacher, and drinking companion. He could also predict the future.

Besides being smart, Silenus was a seer. He could predict the future of anybody who managed to tie him up as he slept after drinking heavily. However, he was not a fool or a comic character, but someone whom the Greeks respected. The great philosopher Plato even complimented his legendary teacher Socrates by comparing him to Silenus.

Pan

Another being who followed Dionysus around was Pan, the god of shepherds. He watched over them and their flocks to assure that no harm would come to them. Pan is usually pictured as a Satyr. He is the son of Hermes, the messenger of the gods.

All the wild places of the world, such as the woods and mountains, were home to Pan. As such, he was the companion of nymphs and others who lived in these places. When they danced, he danced. He usually played his famous pipes by blowing across them. Even though he constantly chased after nymphs, who were young and beautiful, he was usually rejected by them because he was so ugly. In fact, that was the way he supposedly obtained his pipes—he was chasing a nymph who was changed into river reeds in order to avoid him. When the wind blew through these reeds it made a pleasant sound, so Pan cut some of them and made them into a musical instrument.

Pan is the subject of *Idyll*, an 1875 painting by Arnold Böcklin. Pan was often depicted with the face and arms of a human and the legs and horns of a goat.

Pan was also supposedly responsible for the eerie sounds travelers would hear late at night as they were walking along quiet roads. Researchers have concluded that the word *panic* comes from these frightening sounds.

Show Me a Picture

Another interesting thing about Dionysus is the manner in which he was portrayed. Initially, he was shown as an older man wearing a beard and usually a crown of ivy. As he became more popular, his appearance began to change. He became younger and lost the beard. Eventually he became a young man. (Similarly in Rome, Bacchus—the Roman version of Dionysus—was often portrayed as a bearded man, but also sometimes as a youth.) Sometimes Dionysus wore the skin of a panther or fawn. At other times, he was clothed in a long robe of a style commonly worn by women. His hair became longer and curlier. His head remained crowned by ivy, but the ivy was often combined with bunches of grapes. In one hand he was often pictured as holding a wine cup. In his other was a thyrsus. In a sense, he was portrayed as more effeminate (acting like a woman).

Dionysus is the only god who displayed this trait, which may be linked to his possible origins in water. Water is usually considered to be a female element. Even though Greek mythology contains a male god of the sea, Poseidon (poh-SY-dun), virtually all the other water deities are female, such as mermaids, water maidens, and nymphs.

Dionysus was raised by nymphs on Nysa. Then, as he traveled throughout the world spreading his gift of wine and winemaking, his followers were usually female. Whereas the other gods have attendants of their sex, Dionysus, the male, has female followers and worshipers.

Otto writes: "Dionysus is always surrounded by women."[5] He cites a story in which Hermes gives the baby Dionysus to Ino and tells her to raise him as a girl.[6]

Finally, there is the way the god dresses. He was often portrayed as wearing long, flowing robes, more typical to females than males. Thus

Some people see *The Drunkards,* or *The Triumph of Bacchus,* painted around 1629 by Diego Velásquez de Silva, as mocking the deity. Others believe Velásquez was showing how Dionysus, or Bacchus, had conquered the world with wine.

some researchers have concluded that Dionysus has something feminine in his character. It is another aspect of the duality of his nature. On one hand, he is a warrior who defeats his enemies. On the other, he is gentle—almost shy—and seems to want to talk to his foes rather than fight them.

This two-sided nature is illustrated by the actions of the Maenads. They are women and mothers, who are kind and gentle. They risked their lives to bring life into the world when they gave birth to their children. Yet these same women, when frenzied, could very easily take life away, even from their own children. They would rip apart any living creature they encountered.

Edith Hamilton

Anyone who spends any time reading or studying Greek or Roman mythology is certain to come into contact with the name Edith Hamilton. Although her work and writings on the subject are more than sixty years old, they are still considered invaluable.

Hamilton was born on August 12, 1867, in Dresden, Germany, but grew up in Fort Wayne, Indiana, in the United States. When she was just seven years old, her father began teaching her foreign languages, including Latin and Greek. Despite her family's objections, she attended Bryn Mawr College near Philadelphia, Pennsylvania, graduating in 1894 with a master's degree. In 1895, she and one of her sisters, Alice, were the first females accepted at the German universities of Leipzig and Munich.

After her return to America, she became the headmistress of the Bryn Mawr Preparatory School for Girls in Baltimore, Maryland. Upon her retirement from there in 1922, she moved to New York City and began writing about ancient Greece. Interestingly, she had never traveled there, but got much of her information from the classical mythological tales.

THE CLASSIC BESTSELLER

EDITH HAMILTON

MYTHOLOGY

TIMELESS TALES OF GODS AND HEROES

She soon began writing books that compared life in ancient Greece and Rome with modern-day living. In 1942 she published *Mythology* (left), which summarized tales of the ancient gods. The genius of the book was that it related accounts that were often difficult to read in their original form in easy-to-read modern language. With her formidable knowledge of these classic stories, and her exceptional writing skills, Hamilton wrote a book that is still considered one of the most important in the field. It continues to be used by students and scholars alike.

Her work attracted so much attention that she eventually did go to Greece in 1957, when she was ninety years old. She was made an honorary citizen of Athens. She died on May 31, 1963.

In *Bacchus*, by Caravaggio (1595), the god offers viewers a glass of his "gift" to mankind. When the Romans conquered Greece in 146 BCE, they adopted the Greek gods into their own religion. They depicted their god of wine, Bacchus, in a similar fashion to Dionysus. Even after the ancient deities were no longer worshiped, artists continued to use mythological themes in their works.

DIONYSUS

CHAPTER 4

The Festivals of Dionysus

While the Greeks realized and understood the paradoxical nature of both Dionysus and wine drinking, they certainly had no doubts about celebrating the god and all that he stood for. The Greek festival for Dionysus, known as the Dionysia, became legendary.

The Dionysia

The Dionysia was the combined name for two festivals held at different times of the year to honor Dionysus: the rural Dionysia and the city Dionysia. Together, these two festivals became so famous that references to them and what occurred there are still mentioned today.

The rural Dionysia was held during the winter, probably in what would be the month of December today. It was most likely held to celebrate the cultivation of vines. The most important part of the festival was the procession, which was much like a modern-day parade. Those who took part in the procession carried such items as loaves of bread, jars of water and wine, and baskets. There were also singing, dancing, and possibly performances of plays.

The City Dionysia was held about three months after the rural festival, around the end of March to early April. It may have been held to celebrate the end of winter. The city Dionysia was held in Athens, and was the responsibility of the *archon*, which was a government official similar to a mayor.

As with the rural Dionysia, there was a procession as in the city Dionysia, and a feast. However, the most competitive and noteworthy part of the festival was reserved for performing theatrical plays. The plays, both comedies and tragedies, were judged as to which one was best. It was considered quite an honor for a performer or playwright to win a prize at the city Dionysia. The plays were performed at the

The Theater of Dionysus could seat up to 17,000 people. Located at the foot of the Acropolis, it was the site of theatrical competitions held during the city Dionysia.

Theater of Dionysus in Athens. Dionysus was thought to be present at every play. His priest sat in the seat of honor for every performance.

First the tragedies were staged, and then the comedies. The winning play was announced on the last day of the festival. The playwright won a crown of ivy. If the play had been written long ago and the playwright was dead, the crown was given to the producer of the play.

The city Dionysia was an incredibly important event for Greeks for numerous reasons. First of all, it encouraged the writing of plays. The actors, poets, and singers who performed were all thought to be servants of the god. Thus, in effect, performing the plays became an act of worship.

Second, the festival allowed lower-class citizens to behave more freely. For example, in Greek society men usually held power over women and ruled their lives. During the festival, women were free to ridicule their male relatives. Ideas that normally would be silenced, such as those criticizing the government, were allowed to be expressed during a play's performance. Thus the festival allowed those who normally had to stifle their voice to blow off some steam.

The festival of Dionysus represented a break from the ordinary routines of life, and celebration and enjoyment took center stage. As Edith Hamilton explained: "[The festival days] were days of perfect peace and enjoyment. All the ordinary business of life stopped. No one could be put in prison; prisoners were even released so that they could share in the general rejoicing."[1]

The festival of Dionysus was not a religious rite that ended in a temple or with a sacrifice or feast. Instead, the entire festival pointed toward one climatic theatrical event: the writing and performing of plays.

This is not as strange as it may seem. More than any other god, it was thought that Dionysus was felt inside a person, and that his spirit could move a person to do great things. The other gods reacted with people on an external level, but Dionysus did so internally. If the spirit of Dionysus was inside someone, it was entirely possible that they could be inspired to write a great play.

There was a reason that the tragic plays far outweighed the comedies, both in importance and meaning for the festival. As Greek mythology scholars such as Hamilton have pointed out, more than any other god, Dionysus was a tragic figure. He was considered to be like the grapevine for which he was known: Each year, the vine was pruned and cut to almost nothing to help it regenerate and produce vigorous new growth the next year. As the growing season ended and winter's chill fell on the landscape, the pruned grapevine was nothing more than a bare brown stick; it looked incapable of ever living again.

In the same manner, Dionysus was thought to die with the coming of cold weather. Even his childhood was filled with death. The Titans tricked him with toys and then tore him to pieces so that only his heart was left. When Dionysus is viewed like this, it is not surprising that the tragedies were the more important of the plays produced for his festival.

"Dionysus . . . is the suffering god," wrote Otto.[2]

"He was the tragic god," wrote Hamilton. "There was none other."[3]

Yet there is another side to this theme of seasonal death. Even though every year Dionysus died, every year he was reborn, and returned. As Hamilton wrote: "He was the assurance that death does not end all. His worshipers believed that his death and resurrection showed that the soul lives on forever after the body dies. In his resurrection he was the embodiment of the life that is stronger than death. He . . . became the center of the belief in immortality."[4] So even though Dionysus was tragic, his returning to life gave people hope that death was not the end of everything.

Indeed, this idea of the continued existence of the soul was evident throughout the lives of ancient Greeks. Plutarch was one of the most famous of all Greek writers. Around 80 CE he received word that his young daughter had died. In a letter to his wife, he wrote: ". . . that the soul once departed from the body vanishes and feels nothing I know that you give no belief . . . because of those sacred and faithful promises given in the mysteries of Bacchus [Dionysus] which we who are of that religious brotherhood know. We hold it firmly for an undoubted truth that our soul is incorruptible and immortal."[5]

This hopefulness, this confidence that a person's soul lived on and that death was not final, is one of the major reasons why Dionysus was one of the most important, respected, and popular of the Greek gods.

Plutarch

How do modern scholars and researchers know so much about the lives of many of the figures in ancient Greece and Rome thousands of years after they lived, and well before newspapers, cameras, or any other recording devices had been invented? They depend on the writings of ancient scribes. One of the greatest was a Greek writer named Plutarch.

Plutarch was born in 46 BCE, in the town of Chaeronea (ker-un-NEE-uh), which was located in the region of Greece known as Boeotia (bee-OH-shuh). Thanks

Plutarch

to his wealthy parents, he was able to spend much of his time studying philosophy, mathematics, and other subjects at the Academy of Athens.

During his life, Plutarch was a priest, and also a magistrate (judge). He represented his hometown of Chaeronea on trips to other countries. He also had an active social life.

Busy though he was, Plutarch also found plenty of time for writing, and for that modern researchers are grateful. His best-known book is called *Parallel Lives,* a series of biographies of famous Greek and Roman figures. The essays deal as much with character and morality as they tell a straightforward history of the person's life, and that was by design. Plutarch was interested in exploring how a person's character influenced his life. This source has been used by many writers in developing their own books, articles, and plays about figures in the ancient world. For example, Shakespeare used it when he wrote his plays dealing with the Roman Empire, such as *Julius Caesar* and *Antony and Cleopatra.*

Among Plutarch's other works is *Life of Alexander.* This is one of the few surviving descriptions of the famous conqueror, and provides valuable information about him—information that otherwise would probably have been lost.

Plutarch died between 119 and 125 in Chaeronea.

Bacchus and Ariadne, an eighteenth-century painting by Giovanni Battista Pittoni, captures the moment Dionysus meets the abandoned Ariadne. Dionysus and Ariadne eventually get married, and all the gods attend their wedding.

DIONYSUS

CHAPTER 5

The Journeys of Dionysus

As noted earlier, after Dionysus discovered the secret of how to turn grapes into wine, he traveled throughout the world in order to spread this ability among mortals. On these journeys he had many adventures.

New Stars

Descending from the mountains of Thrace, Dionysus entered the country of Attica (the part of the Greek peninsula that includes Athens). There the king, Icarius (ih-KAYR-ee-us), welcomed him. Dionysus rewarded the king for his kindness by giving him vines from which he could obtain grapes and make wine. Icarius did indeed make wine, which he generously gave to his servants. (In other versions of the story, Icarius is just an old man who befriends Dionysus. In gratitude, the god teaches him how to make wine and Icarius goes out to spread this new ability among others.)

At first his servants enjoyed the wine. But the more they drank, the drunker they became and the wilder were their thoughts. Finally, in their drunken state, they became convinced that the king was trying to poison them, so they killed him. (Other versions of the story have Icarius giving wine to shepherds, who also feel as if they are being poisoned and kill Icarius.[1])

Erigone (err-IH-guh-nee), who was Icarius' daughter, went looking for him. She took her loyal dog Maera (or Macra) with her. No matter where Erigone looked, she could not find her father. Finally the dog found Icarius' tomb and brought Erigone to it. The young girl was heartbroken to discover that her father was dead. Depressed, she hanged herself. With both of his masters gone, the dog also killed himself by jumping into a well.

When Dionysus discovered that not only his friend but also his daughter and the dog were dead, he caused all the women of Attica to go insane. The people of Attica consulted an oracle, who told them why this was happening. The people then caught the assassins and punished them, causing Dionysus to lift the madness. He had the bodies of Icarius and Erigone, as well as the dog, brought up to the heavens. There they became the constellations Waggoner (Boötes), Virgo, and Canis Minor (Lesser Dog).

Dionysus Finds Romance

On his journeys, Dionysus encountered romance. When he went to Aetolia (ee-TOH-lee-uh), a region of central Greece, he was welcomed by Oeneus (EE-nee-us), the king of Calydon. Dionysus fell in love with the king's wife, Althaea (al-THAY-uh). Oeneus pretended that he did not realize what was occurring. Dionysus was grateful to him, and gave him a grapevine.

In Titian's *Bacchus and Ariadne*, painted around 1523, the god is accompanied by his retinue.

Dionysus and Althaea had a daughter named Deianeira (dee-yuh-NYE-ruh). She was destined to play a significant role in future events. It was she who accidentally gave her husband, the mighty Heracles (known more commonly by his Roman name, Hercules), a poisoned cloak that killed him.

Dionysus and Althaea did not stay together long, but another woman, the beautiful Ariadne (ayr-ee-AD-nee), became his wife.

One day Dionysus encountered Ariadne sleeping on the beach. When she woke up, she saw the handsome god standing over her. However, she also knew that the hero Theseus (THEE-see-us) had brought her all the way from Crete only to abandon her on the beach. Alone and far from home, she began to cry.

Dionysus comforted her, and gave her wine to drink. Soon the young woman was not sad anymore. She and the god fell in love, and decided to get married. The wedding was a magnificent affair. All the gods came and brought many gifts for the happy couple.

Dionysus and Ariadne had three or four sons, including Oenopion (ee-NOH-pee-on) and Staphylus (STAH-fuh-lus). Oenopion became a king. Staphylus grew up to become one of the legendary Argonauts who joined Jason on his quest for the Golden Fleece.

This is the most popular of the tales about the relationship between Dionysus and Ariadne. Another version of the tale related by Homer says that the young girl was first killed by Artemis, the goddess of the hunt. After her death, she was married to Dionysus.[2]

Dionysus Travels Outside the Greek World
The travels of Dionysus were not limited to the Greek world. He also journeyed outside Greece, traveling to such places as Phrygia, Syria, and Lebanon. He seemed to be on a path that would bring him to Egypt and India, and eventually he did indeed visit those two places. Everywhere he went he spread both civilization and his secret of winemaking. Sometimes he was assisted in his journeys by Zeus, who sent his son a tiger to help him cross the Tigris River; but often Dionysus was equal to the task of solving whatever problem lay before him. For example, when he needed to cross the Euphrates River, he did so by connecting both sides with a heavy vine stalk like a thick rope.

In Libya, Dionysus displayed a fighting side. He helped Ammon, the king, to reclaim his rightful place on his throne after Cronus and the Titans had forced him to run away. There are also tales about how he conquered India, and then taught the people there winemaking.

After he returned to the Greek world from the East, he encountered Lycurgus, the king of Thrace. Lycurgus did not approve of this new god, of wine drinking, or of those who followed this new idea. He decided

In 1760, Francesco de Mura painted Dionysus and his retinue, including Silenus on his donkey (left), Maenads, and satyrs.

to try to destroy Dionysus. He declared that he was against the god, and he imprisoned the Maenads.

Lycurgus was a powerful king, and initially Dionysus was forced to run away from him rather than fight. He chose to escape by diving into the sea.

The god did not hide from Lycurgus forever. Eventually he returned and made all the inhabitants of Thrace sterile (unable to have children). Lycurgus went insane. While out of his mind, the king killed his son, Dryas, because he thought him to be a vine.

Yet even that dreadful act was not vengeance enough for Dionysus. The citizens of Thrace continued to suffer until an oracle told them that their suffering would not end until Lycurgus was dead. They brought

In a seventeenth-century drawing, King Pentheus of Thebes, who wants to stop the worship of Dionysus, is brought to the god. The king would pay for his interference with his life.

him to a mountain, where he was either trampled to death or torn apart by wild horses.

Another ruler who discovered that it was not wise to cross this new god and his followers was Pentheus (PEN-thee-us). He was the ruler of Thebes, a large city in Egypt with seven gates to protect it from intruders and invading armies. When Dionysus arrived there, the people of Thebes began to be afflicted with a new and strange kind of insanity; they left their homes and joined the Maenads and participated in their strange and violent rituals.

Pentheus was outraged. He feared his city would soon be a hollow shell, with virtually no one left in it. In order to stop this, he imprisoned both Dionysus and his followers.

Dionysus easily escaped the mortal prison. Assuming his most charming attitude and mannerisms, he went to see Pentheus. Soon the king who had been his sworn enemy was his friend.

The god used his friendship with Pentheus to convince him to accompany him up to the mountains. Once there, Dionysus said, the king would be able to hide and spy on the Maenads to discover the secrets of what they were doing.

Pentheus was eager to see for himself what was going on, and to discover these secrets. He disguised himself as one of the Maenads and followed Dionysus up to the mountains. Once there, the king climbed a very tall pine tree. He watched, stunned, as the women danced and ate the raw flesh of animals they killed.

In the midst of their celebration, the women discovered Pentheus hiding in the tree. Dionysus created a blue mist that tricked the women into thinking that the king was actually a lion. Savagely, the women attacked Pentheus and tore his body limb from limb.

Among the Maenads on the mountain was Agave (AH-gah-vee), the mother of Pentheus. The blue mist tricked her just as it had tricked everybody else, and she did not realize that she was killing her own son. She picked up the head of Pentheus and put it on the end of her thyrsus. She marched into Thebes, proudly displaying the head.

At that moment, Dionysus removed the influence of the blue mist from her mind, and she realized what she had done. The grief-stricken mother was exiled from the city. Polydorus, Pentheus' uncle, succeeded him as the king of Thebes. Polydorus made Thebes one of the most important centers for worshiping Dionysus and welcoming his followers.

After this experience, it would seem as if the foolish notion of defying Dionysus and resisting his followers should be completely abandoned. But still there were some who did not get the word. Such was the case with the three daughters of King Manyas. When the worship of Dionysus arrived in their homeland, the girls, Alcithoe (al-SIH-thoh-ee), Leucippe (LOO-kih-pee), and Arsippe (AR-sih-pee), refused to participate. They decided to continue with their daily routines.

Angered by their refusal to worship him, Dionysus changed himself into a young maiden and visited them. With gentle reason, he tried to convince them to change their ways. When they refused, Dionysus changed himself into a bull, a lion, and a panther, right in their presence.

The transformations terrified the young women and made them lose their sanity. In their deranged state of mind, they did not understand what they were doing. Leucippe grabbed her infant son and tore him to pieces with her bare hands. Finally, Dionysus transformed them into a mouse, a screech owl, and an owl.[3] (In another version of the tale, they were all changed into bats.)

This story is very similar to another told about women who dared to defy the worship of Dionysus. These were the daughters of Proteus. They were also driven insane by their refusal to participate in the rituals of Dionysus. In their disturbed state of mind, they thought they were cows. Then they murdered and ate their children.

As these stories illustrate, it was impossible to resist Dionysus or the spread of his wine culture. Those who tried to stop him suffered a horrible fate. Eventually the worship of Dionysus and the making and drinking of wine spread all over the world.

But was humanity the better for it, or the worse?

Dionysus and King Midas

Not every story involving Dionysus concerns the spreading of his cult. For example, the god is also associated with the story of King Midas, and therefore with the wealth of African nations.

In the tale, a group of peasants in Phrygia capture a drunken old man. Midas, king of Phrygia, recognizes him as an old and dear friend of Dionysus—Silenus. Midas treats Silenus well, entertaining him with stories and songs. When Midas returns Silenus to Dionysus, the god is so pleased with how his friend was treated that he offers Midas whatever he wishes. The king asks for the power to change whatever he touches into gold.

Although Dionysus thinks that this is a foolish wish, he grants Midas' request. The king quickly finds out that although it might have been wonderful to turn ordinary objects, like stones or blankets, into gold, it was quite another story to turn things like food and water into gold.

Realizing that he would soon starve to death, Midas begged Dionysus to take away his gold-touching power. The god told him to bathe in the Pactolus River. Midas did so, and the power passed from his hands and into the river sand. That is why the sands of that particular river are colored like—and actually contain—gold.

In fact, the river flows near Lydia, which was fabulously wealthy in ancient times. The Lydians were the first to mint gold coins. The wealth of the last king of Lydia, Croesus (around 560–546 BCE), was legendary.

Midas and Bacchus, by Nicolas Poussin, c. 1630

Chapter 1. A Bad Day to Be a Pirate

1. Paul Hamlyn, *Greek Mythology* (London, England: Batchworth Press Limited, 1963), p. 110.

Chapter 2. Lord of the Vine

1. Edith Hamilton, *Mythology* (New York: New American Library, 1989), p. 54.

2. John Pinsent, *Greek Mythology* (London: The Hamlyn Publishing Group Limited, 1969), p. 60.

3. Walter F. Otto, *Dionysus— Myth and Cult* (Bloomington: Indiana University Press, 1965), p. 59.

4. Ibid., p. 63.

5. Ibid., p. 61.

Chapter 3. Origins and Friends

1. Paul Hamlyn, *Greek Mythology* (London, England: Batchworth Press Limited, 1963), p. 112.

2. Ibid., p. 113.

3. Edith Hamilton, *Mythology* (New York: New American Library, 1989), p. 57.

4. Ibid., p. 60.

5. Walter F. Otto, *Dionysus— Myth and Cult* (Bloomington: Indiana University Press, 1965), p. 172.

6. Ibid., p. 176.

Chapter 4. The Fesitvals of Dionysus

1. Edith Hamilton, *Mythology* (New York: New American Library, 1989), p. 61.

2. Walter F. Otto, *Dionysus— Myth and Cult* (Bloomington: Indiana University Press, 1965), p. 180.

3. Hamilton, p. 63.

4. Ibid., p. 62.

5. Ibid., p. 62.

Chapter 5. The Journeys of Dionysus

1. Paul Hamlyn, *Greek Mythology* (London, England: Batchworth Press Limited, 1963), p.110.

2. Ibid., p. 111.

3. Ibid., p. 112.

Books

Evslin, Bernard, *Heroes, Gods, and Monsters of the Greek Myths*. New York: Dell Laurel-Leaf, 2005.

Ferguson, Diana, *Greek Myths & Legends*. New York: Sterling Publications, 2000.

Hoena, B. A. *Athena*. Mankato, Minnesota: Capstone Press, 2003.

Osborne, Mary Pope. *The Land of the Dead*. New York: Hyperion Books for Children, 2002.

Spies, Karen Bornemann. *The Iliad and the Odyssey in Greek Mythology*. Berkeley Heights, New Jersey: Enslow Publishers, 2002.

Works Consulted

Cartledge, Paul. *The Greeks—Crucible of Civilization*. New York: TV Books, L.L.C., 2000.

Graves, Robert. *The Greek Myths*. London, England: Penguin Books, 1992.

Hamilton, Edith. *The Greek Way*. New York: Franklin Watts, Inc., 1958.

———. *Mythology*. New York: New American Library, 1989.

Hamlyn, Paul. *Greek Mythology*. London, England: Batchworth Press Limited, 1963.

Johnston, Alan. *The Emergence of Greece*. New York: E.P. Dutton & Co., Inc., 1976.

Kravitz, David. *Who's Who In Greek and Roman Mythology*. New York: Clarkson N. Potter, Inc., 1975.

Moncrieff, A.R. Hope. *A Treasury of Classical Mythology*. New York: Barnes & Noble Books, 1992.

Otto, Walter F. *Dionysus—Myth and Cult*. Bloomington: Indiana University Press, 1965.

Pinsent, John. *Greek Mythology*. *London:* The Paul Hamlyn Publishing Group Limited, 1969.

Reinhardt, David. *Pirates and Piracy*. New York: Konecky & Konecky, 1997.

On the Internet

Greek Mythology
http://www.mythweb.com/

The Immortals: Greek Mythology
http://messagenet.com/myths/chart.html

Encyclopedia Mythica: Greek mythology
http://www.pantheon.org/areas/mythology/europe/greek/

Thinkquest: Greek Mythology: Gods, Goddesses, Titans and More http://library.thinkquest.org/J0110010/

benefactor (BEH-neh-fak-tur)—A person who gives a benefit.

cavort (kuh-VORT)—To dance about wildly.

contradict (kon-truh-DIKT)—To say the opposite.

deity (DEE-uh-tee)—A god or goddess.

effeminate (eh-FEH-mih-nit)—Soft or feminine in traits or habits.

entity (EN-tih-tee)—Something that is real.

epithet (EH-puh-thet)—A nickname that describes a person or thing.

evolve (ee-VOLV)—To change over time.

flourish (FLOOR-ish)—Thrive.

formidable (for-MIH-dah-bul)—Commanding respect; hard to defeat.

frenzy (FREN-zee)—Wild excitement.

gadfly (GAD-fly)—A fly of various species noted for buzzing about animals and sucking their blood.

heifer (HEH-fer)—A cow that has not produced a calf and is under three years old.

idyllic (eye-DIH-lik)—Extremely happy or peaceful.

migrate (MY-grayt)—To move from one area to another.

paradox (PAYR-uh-doks)—An absurd statement that is possibly true.

passive (PAA-siv)—Not relating to something that might be expected to cause a reaction.

perish (PAYR-ish)—Die.

ransom (RAN-sum)—Money paid to free someone.

retinue (REH-tih-noo)—A group of attendants; posse.

ritual (RIH-choo-ul)—An established procedure for a rite.

Titans (TY-tans)—Ancient gods who used to rule the universe until defeated by Zeus and the other Mount Olympus gods.

vindictive (vin-DIK-tiv)—Wanting revenge.

INDEX